CROWNED
Thoughts
The Evolution of Mindset

INEZ V. WALLS

CROWNED
Thoughts
The Evolution of Mindset

CROWNED Thoughts: The Evolution of Mindset

Copyright © 2019 INEZ V. WALLS

ISBN-13: 978-0-9983676-7-5 (paperback)

LCCN: 2019903409

Unless otherwise indicated, all Scripture quotations are taken from the Holy Bible, New Living Translation, copyright © 1996, 2004, 2015 by Tyndale House Foundation. Used by permission of Tyndale House Publishers, Inc., Carol Stream, Illinois 60188. All rights reserved.

Scripture quotations marked (AMP) are taken from the Amplified Bible, Copyright © 1954, 1958, 1962, 1964, 1965, 1987 by The Lockman Foundation. Used by permission.

"Kujichagulia" written by the author. Originally published online: https://mydailykwanzaa.wordpress.com/self-determination- kujichagulia/

YouTube is a registered trademark of Google, LLC
Instagram is a registered trademark of Instagram, LLC

With a Capital M Publishing Group, LLC
P.O. Box 52656
Durham, NC 27717
www.withacapitalm.com
withacapitalm@gmail.com

Special discounts are available on quantity purchases by corporations, associations, and others. For details, contact the publisher at the address above.

PRINTED IN THE U.S.A.

Dedication

This collection of poems is inspired by my parents.

Lucy and Willie,
May you never feel condemnation or regret, but dance in the light and grace of the Lord. Thank you for stewarding my life the way that you did. It built me.

This collection of poems is a gift to my grandmother.

Granny,
May you rest in peace. May your example and legacy live and be honored through me until our by and by.

This collection of poems is dedicated to my sister.

Adena,
May this book breathe as a living testimony of our victory. May it be an inspirational reminder that God's love and plan worked and is working through it all.

Acknowledgments

Cover Art

A'lexus Newkirk

Marketing

Bria Adams

Editing

Teshome Smith-Murray

Mentorship

Breylon Smith and Arlan Wallace

Contents

1

Our Daughter

She was conceived in mama's womb
And planted in the earth.
A round face, brown eyes filled with grace,
With her soles in the dirt
And her soul flaming.

Hope and balance she was
With every stride.
Trailing her was strength-
Oblivious,
She left it behind.

She was conceived in mama's womb
And birthed into the earth.
Full lips, a steady beat in her hips,
With her sun-lit skin
And light-filled melanin,
Her soul flaming.

Purity and royalty she was
With milky dark coating.
Exuding her was excellence
Without the elation of her knowing.

Because her nation, our nation,
Stripped her of her pride
And the torch of hope she carried in this race
For her race,
Her ancestors and her people.

For this perfidious land mocks her-
Her curls, her kinks,

1

OUR DAUGHTER

Her tribe mocks her sanctity,
Her balance, her skin,
And the honor that rests within her flaming soul.

She was unrecognized promise
And systematic revenge on a people.
She was fortitude
And helplessness.

She was righteousness
And degradation
Since the accouchement of her generation-
Since the day of her conception in mama's womb.

But in her curly perfection,
In her dark royalty
And in her sun kissed paradox,
There rested upon her head a crown,
That no being could disturb.

The world has a way of trying to define you. By 'the world' I mean the systems and paradigms, or ways of thinking that exist in our global community. There's a political paradigm, a racial paradigm, an economic paradigm, a cultural paradigm, and an educational paradigm. There are also systems at work for monetary gain: the clothing and fashion industry, the music industry, the sex industry, and the food industry. There are also the isms: racism, sexism, ageism, and colorism.

All of this seems to be a lot. Most things that I just named are never explained to us. We are just born into them. We are born with a hand of cards and forced to play them. I, for instance, was born into poverty as dark-skinned, female and as African American.

This plight brought about its own set of oppressions and struggles that no one knew how to coach me through. Many of us today are products of the struggle we inherited. The world, the systems and the people that subscribe to the systems, can be a dark place when you yourself are blind. The Bible says we are born into sin and shapen in iniquity. Sin is any external action that our flesh commits against God. Iniquities however are more internal and deal with heart posture. Iniquities deal with the guilt felt for past wrongdoing. This is interesting to me because a lot of the isms that I named definitely cause a sense of guilt in our society. Race, sex, and color have always been topics of oppression. Generation after generation has struggled tirelessly to correct, redirect and recreate these mindsets and repent (completely turn from) these iniquities.

No one ever explained it to me like this. I had always heard we were born into sin and shapen in iniquity, but it seemed to only be a tool to express just how 'bad' I was as a child and how I needed the Lord! Again, I say, no one coached me through the spiritual battle I was born into.

If racism and colorism weren't enough, I was also born into poverty. My parents, in summation, were ill-prepared for a child.

One was addicted to drugs and the other addicted to his own emotional turmoil resulting in violence and incarceration. These examples of life and adulthood were etched into my brain early on as I was often left at home alone, left with strangers, molested, terrified, and confused. At the age of six, I was removed from that situation and placed with my grandmother.

Issues didn't stop as a I tried to enter the education system and my extended family dynamic (the world). Feelings of abandonment and never being enough echoed daily. I was teased for my skin color (colorism) and body type (sex industry). I never felt pretty enough.

All the while, God had His hand on me. Beautiful isn't it? God is never surprised by our situations. In Jeremiah 1:5 He says, "I knew you before I formed you in your mother's womb... Before you were born, I set you apart"! Isn't that amazing? God knew exactly what He was doing when He placed me in these isms and circumstances.

God had a plan. We are born with purpose and promise. God plants us in this world to grow. He knows that what's on the inside of us can completely shift what is outside of us. He knows there's a problem with where you were born and who you were born to. But that's why He sent you! You're his Plan A. You're the remedy.

Often, we look at our family and circumstances growing up as hindrances. The older I get, the more I realize all those things were just a set up for the come up! We like to use our parents and our economic upbringing as crutches for why we cannot succeed. I believe you come to a place in life when parental burden no longer affects you. Yes, having the parents you did and being in the situation you were in gave you a set of challenges others may not have had to face. However, at a point, that no longer matters. God places you here with talents and gifts and salvation through grace. Eventually, the choices you make are no longer contingent upon what your parents do, who they are, or what they say. You become accountable for your own actions. Stop using what happened to you as an excuse! You are a victor through Christ, not a victim. Stop walking around insulting God as if He made a mistake in creating you AND YOUR SITUATION. God is God. Simple as that. He makes no mistakes. He understands and He has a plan to prosper you; "to give you a future and a hope" (Jeremiah 29:11). Grab hold of it.

Receiving Christ as my Lord and Savior in high school was the best thing I could have ever done. It was like a light came on. I know it sounds cliché but you know the song 'Amazing Grace?' One verse says, 'was blind but now I see.' Bro. Literally. It was like I was wearing really dark shades and one day they just came off. I started to see the world and these systems I had subscribed to differently. I started to see people differently. I started to see myself differently. Watch this. I started to hope for a future.

In high school I was a mess. My grandmother passed away at the end of my middle school career and my grief became self harm through damaging relationships, fornication, drug and alcohol abuse, and violence. I would love to say that once I got saved around the end of my junior year all of that went away, but that would be false.

I had always been in the church. My grandmother made sure of that. I was praise dancing and talking with God but I didn't know him fully. I wasn't allowing him into every area of my life. Once I got saved, and the lights came on, although I was still bound by my sin, I did see differently. See, salvation is a mental thing first before it ever becomes behavioral.

I started to think that instead of staying with the guy I was with in my hometown, I could actually go to college. Instead of skipping classes, I could actually do my best and turn in work.

Guys, I didn't know what I was working for. High school graduation, I guess. I couldn't fathom life after that, life in a place that wasn't where I was. But I had hope. I had hope that if I just do what I knew I needed to do, God would lead me.

And that's the thing. Maybe you're reading this and you're new to Christ. I mean, new to actually trying to surrender everything to the Savior and live a righteous life. Baby girl, brotha, you know what you need to do. It's God working in us that gives us the desire and power to do what pleases Him, so He's already told you what you need to do. You know He has. Just step out on faith and do it! For me in high school, it was taking my butt to class! It was doing my work! Sometimes we make righteousness so deep and feel that it is so far away. Its not. Reverend Luther

Gamble in my hometown sang a song that said, 'If you make one step, He'll make two.' We use to sing that song and laugh. It was catchy! But in my ignorance, I didn't grasp the power and revelation that was in it. Seriously. Make a step. Just make a step. God will honor your obedience and meet you there.

Needless to say, I went on to The North Carolina Central University and received a Bachelor's of Education, concentrating in literacy. What? Y'all. I got a degree in something that I always knew I was good at. But when I was in the world… remember, trapped in all those systems, ways of thinking, sin, iniquity, and isms, I couldn't see that the inclination I had toward words would be the ticket I needed to get out of my situation. It was ALWAYS God's plan to liberate me. I was waiting on God, but He was waiting on me! He planted me in the earth with all the tools I needed to overcome the 'world.'

The Bible says in John 16:33, "But take heart, because I have overcome the world." Christ has overcome the world. And Christ lives in us, right? Everything that you think you need to get out of your situation is already within you. Dig for it! I was writing stories and poems at a young age, sitting in the back room of my grandmother's house, tormented by discontentment with the body I was born in, tormented by the memories of my dark past, tears streaming, lying on my face in prayer (I couldn't have been older than 13) asking God to heal my grandmother. Asking God to save me. Asking God to change my mother. Asking God to save my father from that prison and bring him home so that he could take me far away from my current situation. I wish I could go back in time and tell that little girl that God had already saved her 2,000 years ago. Maybe then I would have actually believed the words I wrote in April 2006:

I am me. That won't change. I'm wacky and crazy, too goofy for my age. But I have big dreams. I have goals indeed. I know I can reach them if

I just believe.... I could be a teacher, a model, an actress on TV, a singer, a writer, a poet, maybe. If I believe on the cross, if I believe on Christ, I know He will help me for the rest of my life. No matter which way I turn, no matter which way I go, I know I will see the red carpet and success.

The gift God gave me to write is the very reason I'm able to reach each of you today. God's gift of wording and His idea for this book have become my purpose in this season. I can't help but think that He knew I would be here. He knew I'd be typing these very words and I am so grateful to Him for what He has done in my life. I pray that you invite God into your life as well and all of your situations and mindsets. I know He's a healer and He will turn things around for you. Allow Him to transform your mind with His Word. Allow Him to save your soul with His blood and sacrifice. Allow Him to fix your heart and walk.

Pray: "God, I am a sinner. I am guilty of wrong thought patterns, actions, and disbelief. But on today, God, I pray that you make me over. I believe that you sent your son into this sin sick 'world' and all its systems so that He may save the world. I believe he lived a perfect life that I could not and died in my place. Jesus rose again with power and I am thankful. I receive Him into my heart as my Lord and Savior. Because He lives, I can live also. I can live a life of peace and joy. Give me faith to live as you did, Lord. Remind me that salvation begins with changing my mindset before I can effectively change my behaviors. That the Holy Spirit's job. Open my eyes, O God. Make me holy (set apart) as you are holy. Convict me by your Holy Spirit to discern your Word and what you believe about me over what the world says. Lead me in all that I do. Lead me out of this mentality and situation. I know you can and you will. I love you, Lord. Amen."

2

Stolen

I close my eyes tight and try to remember his voice.
I wish I could run and jump in his arms
But these words in his letter are my only choice.

These words.

Black.
And white.
Still.

I stare at them through eyes filled with tears-
Tears that over the years
Have become habitual.

See,
My father was stolen.

Although only eight,
No words or well wishes could ever negate
The way my hearts sags with fear and hurt
That only steel bars can create.

My grandmother would say,
"He's not sentenced to life,"
But what about mine?

What about MY dreams?

My childhood?
My teens?

The system casted its net so far and wide.
That my little life was uprooted
And now is defined by… in-car-cer-a-tion?

At the time I could barely even spell the word

But apparently society wouldn't pardon me
From the shame and labeling of,
In-car-cer-a-tion?

My little life was uprooted
And now defiled.
Desecrated as if never sacred. My
youth, my mind,
Locked away behind
Steel bars,
Mentally and emotionally scarred.

But 'Big Bank America' keeps going 'round,
Collecting two hundred when passing go
And pushing brown fathers to the corners so,
Like monopoly, they go to jail
Their futures dependent on a roll of a dice,
Bound inside desolate cells
With nothing to do but write—

To me.

Eight years old with his letters of hopes, regrets, and failures in my
hand,
My emptiness and innocence wouldn't allow me to understand,
But, God, how I'd try.
I'd close my eyes and pretend I was with him.
I'd pretend my books of fairytales, love, and magic would somehow prevail
And defeat this cruel immoral system
That robs young girls of protection and esteem-

Years of hugs, goodnight kisses, and sweet dreams.

11

STOLEN

My little life was uprooted then,
A small child unable to defend.
But my voice today,
Strong and intense,

Will tell the story of America's 'law and order'
And it will not be quenched.
I will stand on the mountain tops and scream this piece.

"Fathers are being stolen!"
And this nation is the thief.

It took years to get healing. Growing up without a father, and a mother in my case, was tough. It made me feel like a visitor in my extended family. I was lucky to have grandparents that loved me dearly and expected the best of my sister and I. Although our situation was despairing, my grandparents offered us love. My grandparents offered us hope.

My grandmother would have us sit down, almost weekly, to write to my father. We were six or seven years old! I don't remember learning to read but I do remember how I perfected my writing! The beautiful thing is, if my cousins were at my grandmother's house at that time, they would have to sit down and write my dad too! This provided me with a sense that he was important; that my relationship with him was important. It let me know that he wouldn't be gone always.

Going to school was especially trying. Being around children with complete families made me feel like an outsider. I remember being in kindergarten. My teacher was a very loving lady that smiled all the time. I was so comforted by her smile.

The date was nearing Father's Day and we gathered on the carpet to discuss what we would do as a class for our dads. We talked about making cards, which was exciting to me because I always mailed letters to my dad. I thought a card would be nice.

A little girl in my class began throwing the biggest tantrum saying that she didn't want to get her dad anything. She said she didn't like him. She hated him. The teacher tried consoling her and calming her down. The longer this went on the more frustrated I became. I'm not sure of the details of my monologue but I know I said, "At least you have your dad," or something of the sort.

This sent my teacher into a panic as other kids started asking me where my dad was. I remember her hurried energy as she had us line up for the bathroom. She directed me to go to the office to the counselor.

Having a parent in prison during your childhood makes you develop an orphan mentality. This is crushing because there is nothing you can do about it. It's almost like you were born for this hurt. It's hard to wrap your mind around the purpose and reason for this pain as a child. This is one area in the lives of many that is completely out of their control. The decisions of those before you can have a great impact on your life. These decisions would like to sneak in and choke the life from your dreams and goals and future. You must not allow this!

Incarceration has dramatically impacted communities of color. It is assumed that children born in the 90s are products of drugs and violence. Although this is disturbing, it also holds some finite truth.

In the 80s and 90s, political authorities enforced hard penalties for crime and promised 'law and order.' This movement was detrimental to communities suffering through poverty, oppression, drugs, and racial violence.

No, this is not meant to depress you, but to instead give you perspective. I hope that as you grow you begin to see those who came before you, not as the enemy, but as people; as people who fell into making wrong choices under incomprehensible circumstances and environments. No one makes choices this fatal on purpose. No one wants to cause themselves or future generations pain. I feel that in my story those who came before me fell into self-pity and disillusionment. If you're not careful, these same emotional scars can be passed on to you. Generational curses are real. Do not be afraid to say you don't want to be like your parents. Don't be afraid to say you want to be as healthy as you can for your yourself and for your seed. Seek emotional and mental help if needed. Seek therapy if you feel led. Seek Jesus. He will comfort you like no other and order your steps so that you can change your thinking and make headway against the circumstances dealt to you.

My father made choices that were not ideal before I was born. He even continued these into my early childhood. My father today, has reconciled with his past and with his children. He makes an effort DAILY to live on purpose and make decisions that will benefit his future and mine. There is not a time that I feel I can't come to him for wisdom; as his hoary head and experiences have made him wise. He still references letters he got from me when I was seven or ten. Those letters bridge the gap in our relationship and present conversations.

Yes, I needed my dad during my early adolescence. Though he was away, he made efforts to be with me in his absence such as sending gifts on Christmas and writing letters. I will forever be grateful to him for not disappearing on my sister and I as some fathers do. I will also be forever grateful to my grandmother for opening her heart to him and us, and making sure that our relationship never died.

My father was stolen but I feel that for many of us, our innocence and childhood was stolen as well.

An incarcerated parent is a difficult circumstance for a child. Child abuse, molestation, divorce, death of a parent, rape, adoption, and many other circumstances are also detrimental to the development of a child's mind. I get it. I've literally lived it, but these situations are not the end. So many of us face these things and use them as a tool to measure ourselves, even into adulthood. I know so many people who have faced these things and reference them daily. What? How twisted is that? You replay what happened to you when you were ten as a twenty-something year old human being and you allow it to dictate and control your actions, decisions, your moods, who you love, what job you take, and what you say. It's not healthy. We are not victims of those situations. You cannot view yourself as a victim your entire life. Change your mindset.

I believe if we are ever truly going to get free from what the world told us when we were young or even what the adults in our lives did, we are going to have to change our mindset. You can't change what happened and you can't change people, but you can change yourself. You can change how you choose to react and deal with the situations. External things should not have absolute power over your mental health and well-being.

I had to let go of what my mother did. I had to let go of what my father did. Although I have had these difficult conversations with both of my parents, I also had to be okay with never getting the apology I felt I deserved. Why? I let go because I realized I can't control people. I can't bend the world and time to fit my comfortability and satisfaction. I am not God. God knew all these things would happen and God loves me. I know that may seem contradictory but really listen to what I am saying: God knew these things would happen AND God loves me.

God loves us deeper than we can ever imagine. It pains Him to see us going through things, especially things we have no control over. You couldn't control your parents' divorce. You couldn't control when your father or mother beat you. You couldn't control being given away by your mother before she even took the time to get to know you. You couldn't control the sickness and death. You couldn't control your father walking away. You couldn't control those things. Those things are not your fault. God knows that. He doesn't see you as a product of those situations. He doesn't view you through that lens. Why are you still viewing yourself as merely that? God sees you as wholly loved. He sees you as righteous (that means in right standing with Him if you believe in Jesus Christ). 1 Peter 2:9 says He sees you as, "royal priests, a holy nation, God's very own possession." He sees you as an eternal daughter and son. Bask in that. What God thinks is the only thing that will ever stand. The rest of this will fade away.

Anchor your heart and your mind in what will last. One of the first mental steps I'm going to encourage you to take is to stop looking at yourself through the lens of your childhood, your past, and what happened to you. See yourself through the eyes of Christ. Go to the well that never runs dry. Find or purchase a copy of Scripture. Download an app with Scripture. Read about who you really are. This world is just smoke and mirrors trying to contort what is truth. Start by reading *The Gospel Revealed*, the New Testament: Matthew, Mark, Luke, and John. Jesus died so that you may live in His truth. Learn of Him. Accept Him. Accept who you were created to be.

Pray: 'God, I rebuke the victim mentality that has taken root in my mind. I ask God that you cleanse me of any and all self pity that is hindering me from being the best version of myself. I pray and speak peace over the people who have hurt me. I pray that you forgive them and guide me into forgiveness. I pray that you prosper them and keep them from harm. I pray that they mentally grow and come into the knowledge of Christ. I rebuke any and all condemnation they may feel. I pray strength over their hearts and mine. Heal me, O God, from my past. Teach me who you are so that I may know the comfort of your presence. I accept you into my heart, Lord. I accept who you created me to be, despite what I have been through and those who came before me. In Jesus' name. Amen.'

3

Whispers in the Dark

The room is dark.
My soul is deeper than blue
As I whisper a prayer to you.

My tear-spangled face toward heaven.

Any journey is going to require hard work, dedication and even tears. Anything worth having is worth working for. Diving into who you are and where you come from is only one of many steps toward self-love. I loved getting to know me at my root. Just like a tree, the roots determine the strength and character of who you become.

Digging to find the love and blessings at my root was tough. I remember being in college, in my room late at night, crying insatiably. I wasn't happy. I was in college on a full ride scholarship and I wasn't happy. Imagine that. To make things worse, I felt as if no one would understand my plight. No one would understand how or why I was feeling the way I was feeling. It's not normalcy to self-reflect and go against the grain of who you thought you were to find who you are supposed to be. Do not expect everyone to understand your journey once you embark. It takes a courageous and strong person to look long and hard in the mirror at what is underneath the surface.

At that time, I could not turn to friends or family for consolation. So, in need, I turned to Heaven.

I often times think that we as a people 'sleep' on God. What do I mean? We go through so much and get overwhelmed so often. It's baffling that instead of going to God during those times, we turn to mama and friends. Mama and friends can only influence or change what they can control and they only know you based on their interactions with you. For example, don't you despise going to someone when you're in need of advice or you just want to vent and that person seems clueless as to what you're talking about? You have to spend an half hour backtracking, trying to explain what happened last week and what happened in your dream and what your co-worker said and what the pastor said Sunday JUST so they can be up to speed! It's exhausting! They only know you based on your interaction with them and what information you relay to them.

God on the other hand, God KNOWS you. I mean, really KNOWS you. You don't have to fill Him in on the small details. You don't have to tiptoe around a point because He already gets it. You don't have to replay the incident because He was there! There's a solace in that. It is absolutely freeing to know that you have a friend that will always understand and will always love you through every situation. He will never leave. He is always present and one hundred percent on your side, nudging you toward His greater plan for your life. He comforts you. His Spirit advises you. He wipes your tears, picks you up, and leads you onward.

That is exactly what God did for me that night in my dorm room. I remember whispering to Him that I needed Him. I remember whispering, "It hurts." The shadows of my past, the guilt of shallow decisions, the crying, and now the headache from crying, were all too much. I needed a hug. Ever been there? And like magic, before the thought was even fully conceived, I felt a presence, a wind, enter the room and linger right next to me. I felt so safe and warm. My heart steadied. I smiled and the marks from my tears felt cool on my face. I was at peace.

At such a time as this I feel that we need peace; "God's peace, which exceeds anything we can understand" (Philippians 4:7). So many trials and circumstances can push us to a dark night in a dark room. Not just physically as we end a day, but even as we walk around. Some of us are living with a dark room in our mind. In our mind, there is no light. We are lost. We feel empty. Why? It could be our haunting past. It could anger or resentment. It could even be our discontentment with our portion.

When we face trauma early in life, we are vulnerable. Oftentimes we take a defensive stance against life. Most of how we act, what we say, who we choose to be around, and our beliefs of ourselves stem from a dark and misconstrued place. We start to believe that we are not worthy of love. We internalize that the situation we are in is exactly what we deserve. We subconsciously tear ourselves down at every turn in an effort to 'beat life to the punch.' We would rather self-destruct than give any other human the opportunity to criticize us.

I've been there. The issue with that negative pattern of thinking is that it is toxic. It will spill into every area of your life and before you know it, you're in a dark room crying like life is being choked out of your soul. I don't want anyone to ever have to visit a mental place like that. You don't have to.

I use to tear myself down because of who my parents were. I would tell myself that I wouldn't amount to much because of those who came before me. Who told me that? That thought was not based in fact or reality. I would criticize my own skin tone, hair, and body because I had been ridiculed countlessly by those close to me. For that reason, I was 9, 10, even 11 years old, hating the body God enveloped me in. Any grades I earned or work I would do was never good enough to me. Not because of its quality, but simply because I was the one who did the work! I didn't feel that anything I did was remarkable. Even up into college, I would smite my own hard work, scholarship, and graduation. I knew I had worked very hard for these things, but my negative pattern of thinking and mindset would not let me live! It would not let me breathe in contentment. It constantly catapulted me into a search for better.

I believe it is very healthy to set goals and work toward achieving those goals IF you have actually spent time celebrating where you currently are. It makes no sense to keep chasing after higher and better if you're never going to appreciate the better you are already in. In high school, I couldn't appreciate making good grades, because all I wanted was to graduate. I couldn't appreciate my graduation until I finalized my North Carolina Teaching Fellows Scholarship. Then, I didn't have time to celebrate being a recipient of that scholarship, because I needed to get accepted into the university I desired to attend. That acceptance letter was no good though because I needed to actually take Teacher Education Program courses. And those courses meant nothing if I didn't get my degree on time. What a cycle?!

This unrelenting mindset can be torture for you but look so appealing to others. People would congratulate me and I, in the spirit of humility, would give glory to God. On the inside, however, I was thinking, "Seriously? That was nothing. That was easy. What I really need to be doing is this or I really should be doing that." Do you not understand that obtaining those goals and reaching those milestones are not easy for everyone? Honey, you were gifted and graced for that! I did not realize this at the time of my whisper in the dark. I was too blinded by my pernicious drive for more.

The dark corner in your mind may be different from mine. At that time, mine was discontentment and confusion. Maybe yours is a place of suicidal thoughts or feelings of unworthiness. Maybe yours is a spirit of abandonment or drug and alcohol abuse. No matter what darkness ensues, there is always a light that can drive it away.

"A man's chief happiness is to be what he is." This quote was used in a book called, "365 Days of Wonder: Mr. Browne's Book of Precepts." It is an extension of the precepts, or words to live by, used in the popular novel and movie "Wonder" by R.J. Palacio. I use the book in my classroom to teach character. This one quote, however, really stuck with me. When you feel that you are unhappy with your portion, unhappy with the course your life has taken, or not satisfied with your achievements, stop and remember who God is. He's your creator. He doesn't make mistakes. You are His accomplishment because you believe. He didn't create you on a bad day. You're not living a bad life. Connect with your creator and you'll connect with who and what you are.

This does not come overnight. This is a spiritual connection. It's so hard for us as millennials to make spiritual connections. It's so much easier to make social connections and media connections. We can connect with our favorite blogger or Youtuber, we can even connect with a new bae on a dating site, but when it comes to connecting with God, we freeze. It's not tangible. It's not measurable. We can't open an app to see what He's up to. We can't read His thoughts and retweet them. We can't comment on His most recent post to let Him know we agree. We literally have to stop and put everything else down and focus on Him. We have to be at His feet. This means bowed before Him in prayer, longing to hear His voice and feel His presence. When we get into the habit of doing this and actually build a relationship with God, that connection will become our chief happiness because it will reveal blessings, grace, and favor in us that we never knew existed. In those moments with God we can simply be; just be His sons and daughters.

God is our father. God is our best friend. It's an amazing revelation to know that during your dark times, God didn't leave you. God is constant. He didn't give up. He didn't fail… we did. His love and grace and might didn't change… we changed. We decided to look more at our situation than at God. We decided to trust what we can see more than we trust the invisible God that created it all.

If God is intentional and constructed every detail of our life, it had to have been his plan for us to overcome it all. Even after we slipped up and gave more credit to the devil than he deserved, God is still right there to accept us and love us. So we can't really complain. I personally have witnessed God lift me out of the dark places of my life and dark corners of my mind into so much joy and peace. The good news is that if He's done it before, He'll do it again. The sacrifice He made on the cross is permanent and it reaches to every unbearable situation we find ourselves in. Jesus died so that we may have life. Not a tormented life. Not a depressed life or a life hijacked by obsessive thoughts. He wants us to live spiritually, emotionally, and mentally free.

One practical way to become free is by monitoring what you are allowing to speak into your life. This includes people, conversations, music, TV shows, movies, etc.

Remember, evolution starts with your mindset. It will be difficult to take behavioral steps toward evolution if you haven't yet accepted a different way of looking at your situation.

When I prayed to God to ask Him to help me keep my mind on Him, He provided simple ways to do so. We can keep our minds in worship and make sure that we aren't getting distracted by the world by filtering what we listen to. A musical fast can be helpful. It totally helped me. I love music with culturally relevant message and tons of bass! There's certain types of music that sparks my writing and creativity, however, I have to put those things down when I'm taking a musical fast. I have to monitor what and who is pouring into me. If God is the head of my life, HE should be leading me and inspiring me. I should be meditating on HIS words. I should be listening to HIS voice. Music with messages of salvation and surrender would be greatly beneficial in a season of confusion and desperation for His presence and help.

Podcasts of sermons or even sermons on YouTube can lift you from that dark place as well. I suggest you find a preacher, man or woman of God, that you enjoy listening to and that you vibe with. Watch YouTube like you watch Netflix or any other streaming service! My YouTube is constantly suggesting worship music and sermons. I have subscribed and have certain churches and pastors on my queue. I constantly have a word to listen to instead of watching some crazy show that gives me nightmares and plants doubt and fear in my heart.

Become best buds with Jesus. Yes, it sounds funny but seriously… include him in your leisure activities. "Well, Inez, that sounds great, but is it realistic?" Honestly guys, I don't listen to Christian and worship music all day long and I don't only watch sermons. But trust me, for a period of time, try it. Go on a periodic fast wherein you only listen to Christian music and watch sermons or Christian movies. You don't have to be laid out in worship every day either. I was at first and it was lit, but that doesn't have to be your path! Look up different artists such as Lecrae and Andy Mineo if you're missing your trap beats. Look into Jonathan McReynolds and Mali Music for a more soulful feel. If you're a rock fan, Toby Mac is amazing! Tori Kelly and Tauren Wells are amazing if you're feeling a little pop. Swing back home on Sunday mornings with your Kirk and Yolanda and lay out in worship with Bethel and Hillsong at night. Y'all, incorporate God. He wants to be near you. Filtering out all the world's mess just to be closer to Him pleases Him. Draw nearer to God and He'll draw nearer to you. You will hear His voice and feel His presence; the darkness will flee.

I encourage you not to 'sleep' on God. He's already with you. Call out to Him when you don't understand or when you are lost. Clear your mind from the junk that is trying to overtake your thought life (the life you live in your head that no one else can hear). Call on Jesus when you feel desolate. God cares and He answers. Even if you don't know what to pray, He hears your heart. A faint but desperate whisper in the dark could change your life.

The Bible says, "*The Lord hears his people when they call to him for help. He rescues them from all their troubles. The Lord is close to the brokenhearted; he rescues those whose spirits are crushed. The righteous person faces many troubles, but the Lord comes to the rescue each time.*" (Psalms 34:17-19).

Pray: 'Lord, I know that you hear me when I call. Teach me to call on you in all circumstances. Teach me to rely on you as my Savior. Take over the thoughts that try to take over my psyche. Keep me in a place of desperation to hear your voice and follow your voice alone. I don't want to 'sleep' on you, God. I want to know you as my Father and my friend. I come against depression and anxiety right now in the name of Jesus. I break strongholds of the mind that have kept me down. I release peace and confidence. I come into agreement with heaven and say that I shall live and not die. By the power of the Holy Spirit, it is so. Amen.'

4

What We Broke Ourselves For

"Stand up straight,
Close your legs when you sit.
Don't burp out loud and don't spit.

Do something to your head, child.
Put down that ball.
Learn to walk in heels-
Don't you dare fall!

You talk too much.
You're goofy and
You better learn to cook if you want a husband."

'But I do want a husband,'
The words echo in my broken soul
Like a rhythm and blues crooner.

I do, so I break and bend,
But the emptiness never ends.
At a young age deciding which dress is too tight
And which skirt would fit just right.

Learning to be seen and not heard as if it's a child's place,
When really the command was a verbal slap in the face
To my femininity.
Although never verbatim,

Questions like, "Where's your boyfriend this
Thanksgiving?"
Sneakily encourages you to date him-
Lie down, but not to dream,
Instead to be overcome with what is not, but seems-
Lust, masked as love;
The false admiration thereof.

Broken.
Smiling ear to ear.
Broken.
Year after year trying to remember what you broke yourself for.
Not love or affection.
Time spent going in the wrong direction
"Finding yourself" in early childhood
As if your value equates to that of a doll,
Like a toy a child drops in the mall
Just to realize you were never lost,
Just broken.
And all you have to do is rebuild.

In this epiphany I walk with my head held high
To the beat of the drum I hear in my mind
Because, baby, I bump
Like the bass of hip hop,
I'm beautiful and inspiring with every thought.

I grew up.
I am not quiet.
My charismatic soul and dreams are so loud,
You have to plug your ears to ignore the sound.

Now looking in the mirror
Staring back is the most beautiful brown,
Brown eyes, bright smile, lips full and round,

And upon my head, the most beautiful crown.

And for the life of me,
I cannot remember what I broke myself for.

God has given us purpose; a reason for being on this earth.
Chiefly, our purpose is to worship Him. Then, we honor Him and
bring Him glory through an individual purpose. This purpose is
fueled by the gifts, passions, and talents we possess. This purpose
requires work. We have to work the gift. We have to exercise our
God-given passions. We have to showcase our talents.

God has also created us with personality; a combination of
qualities that form our character. Our personality may be our most
difficult battle when it comes to submitting to the will of God for
our lives. A lot of us are led by our earthly passions that are birthed
from our personalities.

You may be a wild flower or a laid back soul. You may love
anime or music or even poetry. These passions are fueled by your
personality. When you find the things you are interested in, you
hold fast to them, feeling a sense of comfort. In Matthew 6:33
(AMP) God commands us to "first and most importantly seek
(aim at, strive after) His kingdom and His righteousness [His way
of doing and being right— the attitude and character of God], and
all these things will be given to you also." If we are constantly
chasing after earthly passions, when are we taking time to seek
God's face? These earthly passions should be checked. Is this
Spirit led? Is this an avenue by which I can bring God glory?

In the Bible we see that the disciples all had different
personalities, just as we do today. Peter was a firecracker! He was
a firecracker before he met Christ and his personality continued
to shine through during his walk with Christ.

A lot of times, we feel guilty about our personalities.

In the world, we were the life of the party or we were the girl that said whatever was on her mind. Sometimes, we were the 'friend who dropped knowledge on you' randomly during a smoke session or even the person that consoled our heartbroken friend after a lusty relationship came to an end. Either way, we all had a personality that people could identify with and much of our relationships are built on that. God is saying, "I created you. You do not have to hide who you are."

I believe there is this false notion that once you pick up your cross and follow Jesus, you have to suppress who you are. This could not be further from the truth. You crucify your flesh and die to your sin, you don't abandon how God fashioned you. I strongly believe that your personality and who you are will draw a specific crowd of people to your witness. We can't all reach all, meaning: You, specifically, will not be able to bring certain people to Christ. They don't vibe with you. They don't identify with your story. Your story coupled with your personality becomes your testimony; the very testimony that will draw your peers to Christ asking, "What must I do to be saved?"

Personality is something we should embrace! However, we also must remain aware of the fact that personality flaws are real. There's a reason the Bible says in Ephesians 2:8 (AMP), "For it is by grace [God's remarkable compassion and favor drawing you to Christ] that you have been saved [actually delivered from judgement and given eternal life] through faith." We did not have it all together! We were missing a major piece of who we are...The Creator! The very God that created your personality wishes to perfect it.

This is where 'dying to yourself' comes in. This means letting go of who you thought you were to determine who you were meant to be.

I'm a strong believer in self-reflection. I believe in a never ending cycle of learning who I am so that I may work on myself to become my best self, get it? I've gone to therapy, read books, and have taken various personality tests. One specific test was eye opening! I learned that I have an achiever personality. Sounds cool, right? It means that I am constantly living a life of goal setting and goal getting. My zest for life is contagious and people all around me are inspired.

With this radiant personality comes flaws. I've learned that much of my 'zest' is an act. I'm great at projecting an image of happiness and contentment, but in actuality I'm unhappy. In actuality I become depressed when goals seem too far away. I get anxious when I don't understand and I don't actually plan my every step. I procrastinate BIG TIME but my personality projects perfection. I seem like I have all the answers and am confidently living this life without a wrinkle, but truly I only feel as worthy as the compliments and head nods I receive.

The Achiever personality is fueled by external validation. Due to my negative pattern of thinking, I need people to tell me I'm great in order to feel great. I need people to tell me I'm loved in order to feel loved. I need people to admire my life in order to feel like living it.

Of course, when I first read this test I was shocked by how deeply it read into my personality. These are feelings and attitudes for which I never had language.

These were simply the gears turning in my mind and heart that steered every decision, smile, and accomplishment. I cannot say that I did not know they existed, because I did— in part. I've been self-reflecting since I was in undergrad at The North Carolina Central University. Little did I know; my realizations then were only the tip of the iceberg when it came to my personality flaws.

All in all, I'm a mess! Do you see where grace comes in? My personality drew people to me and helped me make decisions to get where I am today. It has fostered positive relationships with my family. It has gained me friends that are supportive and loving. However, the flaws in my personality cannot be ignored. I think we get in trouble when we start to say "I am who I am" and refuse to change or explore how we can grow.

With the help of the Holy Spirit, I stopped drinking liquor and smoking and cursing. These things were all external; things that I could project to the world to say, "I have it all together." Internal things, however, are harder to reach. This is where we must learn the heart of Jesus. Yes, we must know Him but knowing Him is not where it stops. We must then begin to emulate His love and the way He lived.

This follows a heart change. Notice I did not say personality change. God created that personality and He makes no mistakes. As young Christians, we get swept away in trying to be like grandma, mama, or that deacon in our church instead of being ourselves. This leads our generation to feeling like 'this whole church thing isn't for me.' Instead we must embrace what we bring to the table and lay it all at God's feet.

Pray: "Lord, I give all of who I am to you. I pray that you will use me, my talent and my personality for YOUR glory, not my own. Amen."

5

A Season of Letting Go

A gentle breeze pans across the vivid sky.
A bare tree sways, and before my eyes
I see the last maroon leaf crumble then fly.
It flutters slowly to the misty ground
And without making a sound
Settles amongst the others.

My cheeks grow warm and there's a lump in my throat.
You see, this tree and I, we're in the same boat.
We're stripped.
And left standing alone, vulnerable,
With no one to call and no one to hold.

They say
To everything there is a season.
Well, this?
This is a season to cry and a season to mourn
Because no matter how hard I try, I can't bring back the joy

The joy heard in your laugh or the warmth of your touch, I can't bring
back the passion we shared

Although I loved you so much.

See,

Like the leaves on that bare tree, before my eyes

Every piece of us crumbled until you were free to fly-

And you flew.

In an effort not to sound bitter I'll say,

'She's lucky to have you.'

To have the glint of your smile, the delicacy of your kiss,

The scent of your cologne and the bass of your hello,

This agonizing list

In my mind grows longer

As I stand amongst these brittle autumn leaves.

I wipe my eyes and before turning to go,

I glance once more at the bare tree and I notice...

It's not crying with me.

To everything there is a season but somehow this tree knows

You don't have to <u>die</u> in a season of letting go.

Although the leaves left, this tree didn't die.

It still stands firm and beautiful,

Its branches still reach for the sky.

It may look different but nothing has changed.

I step closer—

Its bark is the same!

Its trunk is still planted

And beneath the earth

Its roots are unbothered, steadfast and preparing to birth

POWER in this next period like you've never seen before.

See, right now I'm alone and bare in this season

But this isolation isn't for no reason,

I'm healing, out with the old

So I can tend to my beautiful soul.

See, at my root, I am POWER

And the joke's on you because you coward

Away from this love.

And now the only thing I'm dreaming of

Is a new beginning.

Once the season turns
And a leaf falls,
I hope you know it cannot flutter back up to the tree with

Texts, 'I miss you's, or late night phone calls.
It cannot make it right or ask for grace,
It cannot reappear with a 'sorry' and try to take back its place
Because to everything there is a season,
And baby, you missed your date.

So sit back and watch!
Because at my root, I am POWER.
And after these April showers
I will bloom with leaves and colors green and new,
Vibrant, full of life and virtue,
So, I smile.

Satisfied with this thought and epiphany,
I turn from the bare tree
And gaze at the fallen autumn colors beneath my feet.
I inhale the sweet smell of the season as the crisp breeze flows
Reminding me,
There is a liberating beauty in letting go.

Only God can satisfy you. Cliché, huh?

This statement is absolutely true. God is a well of living water that will never run dry. In other words, God's love is everlasting. We can run to Him and recharge, reset, and renew. He is all that we need to fulfill our lives and the voids that people and things may bring.

How did those voids get there in the first place? At a young age we ran to people and things to fulfill us. Whether toys or boyfriends, we were not okay unless we had them. As we got older, certain shoes, cars and money became our vice. In this generation, a college acceptance letter will let us know whether or not we are worthy. After college? A job offer with a decent salary, an apartment and a significant other does the trick. Guys, all of these things are perishable. More than likely, they will not last long, not if we're obtaining them outside of God's will and God's timing.

I have been the victim, more than a few times, of the consequences of running ahead of God's timing. His timing is perfect. He says in Isaiah 55:8, "'My thoughts are nothing like your thoughts,' says the Lord. 'And my ways are far beyond anything you could imagine.'" This is tough to grapple with. You mean to tell me I'm living this life daily but it's not my own? I don't actually understand it? No, sugar… it's not and you don't. You'll never fully understand. This life belongs to God. Every breath we breathe is because God loved us so much that He gave His only begotten son to die for our sins so that we may live a life that is truly life. What do I mean by that? I mean a life of fulfillment,

TRUE fulfillment that will never expire.

Because we are in this world, we run to worldly fulfillment for our passions. If we're hungry for acceptance, we run to people. If we are hungry for accomplishment, we run to colleges and titles. If we are hungry for good music, we run to secular artists. If we are hungry for spoken word, we run to lustful poetry dens. If we are hungry for intellect, we run to the internet and podcasts that teach lies and brew doubt. If we are hungry for companionship, we run to that friend that is a bad influence or even that guy that only wants one thing.

Too often, friends, we run to things to satisfy us outside of God. Some of the things, we feel, are harmless but if you could peek into the spiritual realm, you would see all of the danger. This is why it's important to have the Holy Spirit lead and guide you. If you have not been baptized by the Holy Spirit, I strongly suggest that you close your eyes and ask the Spirit of God to fill your temple, fill your heart and your mind, and guide you daily as you strive to be more like Christ and bring glory to the Kingdom of God. This Spirit, the Holy Spirit, is a teacher. He also is a counselor. He's the friend that eternally tells you the truth about your life and your mess. A few times, the Holy Spirit has brought people and things to my attention that were not good for me or good for others. I had to heed that message and walk away from some people and things. Was it easy? No. Of course not. But I die to myself so that God may get the glory in everything I do. I trust that He has plans to prosper me and give me a future. I'm not too sure about the durability of any future I could create for myself, so I surrender my daily decision making to Him.

Letting go is tough. In this generation we always say we're 'cutting people off' but rarely do it. It's hard to end relationships with day ones or let birdie fly that doesn't mean us well, but there's one thing I know: We all must go through a season of letting go. God wants all of us! If we've been filling ourselves with things and people instead of Him, He will be jealous. We're so filled up and fat off 'the world' that we have no room to receive His goodness or glory.

I know it hurts. I know the hurt of rejection, abandonment, dishonesty and disloyalty stings. I know he hurt you. I know what mama or daddy did is horrific. I know 'friends' said things that still echo in your mind and tears are the only logical response. However, YOU MUST LET GO. Let go and forgive those that have done you wrong. Once you let go and give it to Jesus, don't go back and vengefully try to pick it up.

Romans 12:21 says, "Don't let evil conquer you, but conquer evil by doing good."

This simply means be kind. Display fruits of the spirit even when it is hard. Be good. Simply be good. The actions of another should not dictate your own. You are in control of your life. You have the ability to turn to Jesus and rest in His peace and love. Retaliating against that person is sinning toward God. Do not allow your anger or hurt to drive a wedge between you and the cross you must bear. Instead give it all to Jesus. He knows and He understands.

All of this is a lot. It's tough to let go of things and people and situations that you feel you must control. 'Rome wasn't built in a day' and neither is holiness. Holiness means to be set apart, different from 'the world.' Paul says in Philippians 3:12, "I don't mean to say that I have already achieved these things or that I have already reached perfection. But I press on to possess that perfection for which Christ Jesus first possessed me." We have to work out our salvation. We PRESS toward the mark perfection. Paul never said we get to the mark. In our flesh, we have to press toward holiness and righteousness and a pressing isn't easy. It takes some strength and time.

So, sis, take the time. One of the most powerful lines of this chapter's poem is, "I'm healing, out with the old so I can tend to my beautiful soul." Take the time necessary for soul healing. Once we've been offended or rejected we tend to pick up every anxiety and issue and go running elsewhere thinking we can escape those negative feelings. The problem is that we run into another job, relationship, or season with the same hurts, issues, and mess.

Again I say, take the time. You have to heal.

I love football. My favorite National Football League team had one of the most accurate kickers in 2017-2018 season. Now this guy is bad! I often times brag about his field goal accuracy to opposing teams. His field goal average is second best in NFL history!

This kicker, however, suffered an injury. This injury during the 2017 season caused him to miss four games. That hurt! But what hurt even worse was his return. When he returned from his injury, his accuracy plummeted. He didn't kick the same. The ball wasn't getting between the uprights. Um, major issue! Sir, you have one job!

The team ended up releasing the kicker before his contract

was complete. Sad story. I was upset.

When I heard the news, the first thing I thought was, 'He wasn't ready.'

The team did not give their kicker enough time to heal. They allowed him to sit down for a while, but then quickly threw him back into the swing of things before he had wholly recovered. The kicker began trying to be a master through pain and it did not work.

What am I saying? You cannot be a master through pain. If you've been injured, if you're hurting, you can't perform at your highest and best. The misconception is that if I'm hurting, I have to push through it. I have to look past my emotional and mental well-being and be what people expect of me.

What? Girl, no. If I could have spoken to that NFL kicker last year before he ran onto the field five games after his injury I would have said, 'Take that helmet off and go home. Rest! Work on you!'

There's not anyone in our corner telling us it's okay to say 'no' to everybody and 'yes' to ourselves. We run ourselves crazy trying to be all that people expect. We run ourselves crazy trying to prove that we are alright when in actuality we are going through.

Healing is a process. It's going to take time. Step away from that committee, that person, your family— you don't have to go to that next meeting. If your friend is trying to set you up on a date, don't go. Getting with another guy is not going to help you get over the other one. Jumping into another bad business venture is not going to help you bounce back from the last one.

Sit with God.

I was doing a lot of writing a year ago. I was doing a lot of studying and I was recording devotions as well. People were giving so much positive feedback. They felt that my words were encouraging and teaching them more about the nature of God and His plan for them.

All the while, I was depressed. I was depressed and anxious about my tomorrow. I was anxious about my purpose and where God was leading me. I was angry. I had built up anger I hadn't dealt with that was coming out at my job. I was discontent. I was 'lonely.' I felt that God was far away.

Okay, the argument here would be that in this scenario I should have just kept pushing forward because God was still working through me.

No, honey, the truth of the matter is that God is tired of using us and not saving us.

God let me know that He's not concerned solely on what I can do for Him. He's concerned about my heart. He told me that those same people who needed my gift now will still be there after I take time away and get whole. It reminded me of the story in Matthew 26 when Jesus told his disciples, "You will always have the poor among you, but you will not always have me."

Jesus wanted me at His feet. He wanted to heal me. He wanted to make me whole. It's His desire that I prosper here on earth. It's His desire that I know the joy of the Lord. It's His desire that I give my all as a living sacrifice, holy and acceptable. How can I do that running on a spiritual 'E'?

It was my twenty-fifth birthday when all of this was coming

to a head. I got on my face and prayed to God and journaled all that He placed on my heart. You see, I was looking for some instructions. I know who the Holy Spirit is and I know that He came to guide me. At my lowest point, I picked myself up from the ground long enough to say, 'Jesus I need you. What would you have me to do?'

During that season, I deleted all social media for the remainder of the year. I stopped calling certain people for advice and forced myself to only call on people I knew lived by the standard of God's Word. I separated myself from unbelievers for a season. I prayed more and read my bible more. That sounds dull but when you have no social media on your phone, what else are you going to check? The Bible App! I made sure it sent me notifications so instead of seeing how somebody else's life was going, I clicked on the Bible App to read about Jesus' life!

Because I was only calling Bible-believing, Christ-followers, I had a lot more intercessory prayer and fellowship. I opened up to let them know what was going on in my heart. I went to church more and actually went to the altar for what I needed! I worshipped and fasted. I also went to therapy.

I know that many people cringe at the thought of psychotherapy but pray about it. See if it's something God would have you to do. I found it as a tool for healing. It was like I was able to talk out my innermost fears and thoughts and have an unbiased person give me practical feedback and steps towards remedy.

I also stopped spending on unnecessary things. Money was a root of my anxiety so I stopped getting my hair and nails done and started doing them myself. Then, I found a great Christian friend to move in with so that my rent and bills could decrease nearly 50%.

Y'all, when I say that was so uncomfortable, I mean it! The whole summer season of 2018 was UNCOMFORTABLE! But I'll tell you this, I grew more in those 6-7 months than I ever have in my life! I grew mentally, emotionally, and spiritually. I went to a Women's Conference in Atlanta, Georgia to reboot. I took time to read about my personality, my God, and my eternal reward. I studied Psalms 23, Hebrews, James, friendship, generosity and debt-freedom. I got more involved and organized within a women's group in my city. I signed up to serve at church and began volunteering at a pregnancy care center. I reconciled with family and co-workers and talked through offenses. I strived to know God in Spirit and in truth; in intimacy and in knowledge.

You're probably thinking, 'That's too much. I ain't got time for all that.' Listen, if you get frustrated enough, you'll change. I had so many voids that I needed to fill with Christ and Christ-centered activities and people. Once you get tired, I mean really tired of those tears, you'll wipe them away and get up on a mission. I was on a mission to be healed. I was on a mission to know God like never before. I knew who I was in Christ and I was TIRED of being mocked by the devil because that's all it was; an attack from the enemy.

A lot of times we are at war with the enemy, this world, and our flesh. We get overtaken by its evils, stresses, fears and anxieties. All of that can change. It can change because the battle has already been won. You have the victory. Will you be bold enough to stand up and fight for it? Will you go looking for it? Will you declare war on your circumstance and your flesh? We're not called 'the army of the Lord' for no reason.

In this next season, fight. Let go then fight!

Pray: 'Lord, I surrender all to you. Lord, I'm tired of fighting this in my own flesh. Empower me to let go of anything that does not please you. Empower me to let go of anyone that doesn't glorify you with their life. Help me God, to love you deeper than I ever have. I know that you can give me the will and power to do what pleases you so intervene, God. Interrupt my plans. Arrest my heart and make it like yours. Guide me by your Spirit. Draw me nearer, O God, so that I may depend on you and not this world. I let go. In Jesus name I am healed and I am free. I have victory in you. Amen.'

6

Now What?

Now what?
Is this all there is?
We've fought and we've pushed.
We've fought and we've pushed-
Now what?

We run, but we're running in circles.
We move the moon and the stars
Just to look up and wonder where we are.

I think we all get to a place where we feel like, "Okay, God. I've done what you've asked of me. Now what?"

Trusting God is tough. Trusting God when you can't see is even more of a challenge. Sometimes we know exactly what God has asked us to do and exactly where He is taking us. We go in for an interview and it goes well. We go to a car lot and we get approved. That family member sits us down and apologizes. That toxic friend dismisses themselves from our lives (really that's God doing the dismissing). We lose the weight. We get the promotion. Those instances are easy to see and trust that God is moving.

What about times when things are falling apart? In the previous chapter, I talked about how falling apart does not mean the end. Often times when we as people feel that life is crumbling, we retreat. Retreating is different for everyone. For me, it means that I take back all the 'stuff' I surrendered to God. I take it back because I need to feel like I'm in control.

A lot of times we are holding blessings that don't belong to us; but because they are so close, we feel that they are ours and under our sole control. What do I mean? God has entrusted you with that child, that man, that job, that dream, and that talent. That does not mean that it belongs to you. Your job is to steward those things well until the day Jesus Christ returns.

Are we stewarding well or are we complaining and trying to give back all that God has blessed us with?

I recently learned how to play poker. A few friends taught me during a cabin trip in the North Carolina mountains. An interesting part of this game is called folding. Folding is when you don't feel confident enough in your cards to continue playing. You throw them in, losing whatever chips you've placed thus far and sit in wait of the outcome for someone else.

While playing this game I folded. The remarkable thing is that once the hand was over and cards were shown, I realized I could have won! I didn't have enough faith in the two little cards in my hand so I threw them in. They weren't enough in my eyes.

This is exactly how we treat our portion, seasons, gifts, and talents. God calls us to do something and sometimes we enjoy the process. Then we get challenged. Then we get blindsided. We begin to look at the cards we are dealt and doubt if God can really come through on His promise. See, we thought we had two pairs or a straight and now it doesn't look like that's going to come to fruition based on what we know.

Based on what YOU know? Do you not understand that God is the Alpha and Omega? He is the creator. "And we know that God causes everything to work together for the good of those who love God and are called according to his purpose for them" (Romans 8:28). He considers all things before giving you that hand. He knows your portion, your bank account, your family, and your gifts. He prepared you for the season that you're in. You don't need to see where you are going. You don't need to see the finish line. Just keep walking.

There is a Mali Music song called, "Walking Shoes." I love Mali Music because his Christian songs have an underground R&B feel. (If you're looking for a positive artist to replace the lusty music you listen to, there you go!). The song "Walking Shoes" talks about continuing to walk even when you don't know where you're going. Knowing that you'll be okay wherever God leads you is a gift. It's a gift you have to work at. How can you blindly trust someone enough to follow them if you don't even know them?

I believe a lack of trust in God is a reflection of our belief in Him. Heavy, right? It's hard to think that you don't believe in God as much as you proclaim. If you truly believe Jesus died on the cross for you; that He stood in the gap for you, you would trust that He has good plans in mind for you. You would trust that He knows what He's doing and just like the cross, He has an end in mind. He has glory in mind. He has love in mind. If you truly know Him, you know that He is the only one who knows who you were, who you are, and who you are going to become.

Remember all of the nights you cried as a child missing your family member who was in prison or that moved away? Remember your tears as your parents separated? Remember when you cried out to Him confused with the direction of your life and bad decisions then He rescued you? Remember when He whispered for you to be obedient to Him and when you stepped out on faith, He protected you and guided you to freedom in a new season? Friend, this time is no different.

I think when we have walked with Jesus and are beginning to access His graces and mercies, we get confident. Rightly so. You should be bold in Christ. However, you also have to remain surrendered. Every season is not the same. Just because doors swung open for you in the past, doesn't mean that now you will not have to work to open another. God is edifying you. He is pruning you for what He has promised you. And growth, guys, is slow. Children grow slowly, plants grow slowly, even hair grows slowly! If you give up on the process, you'll never see the fruit.

Isn't that what we want? We want the promises of God. We want the breakthrough. Notice the word says 'break' and 'through.' Breaking through anything is not easy. It takes effort. It may even take a little injury. Think of trying to punch through a glass. The glass won't crumble on its own so you have to crumble it by it by force. You may injure your hand trying to shatter it. Are you willing to go through that pain to get to the other side?

I know, I know. It's hard. It's tough. You're tired. You don't understand. Other people are getting married and moving and seem happier than you. I know you are getting older. I know you had a plan. But sis, rest in God's plan. Get more spiritual. Do not only believe in what you can see. Believe in the God that's bigger than this physical realm. Believe that He created that moon and those stars that you so desperately want to move. Be sensitive to His spirit and don't move out of His timing.

I can remember a specific time that I definitely moved outside of God's timing. I started to idolize the thought of my future and the enemy used that unfocused time to create a (spiritually) deadly situation.

At this particular time, I was suffering from baby fever. You know, that time in your mid to late twenties when you begin to hope and long for a family. Yes, babies are fussy and require hard work but in the haze of baby fever, they are all you can think about. I allowed myself to sit in that feverish stage for too long. I began to idolize the idea of a family and a child. This is dangerous— very dangerous. See, I was walking right into the devil's playground. His playground is a realm of discontentment and selfish desire. I ended up having sex with someone who wouldn't in a million years be godly husband material. I immediately felt terrible about what I had done to my covenant with the Lord. I chose this guy over Him.

I know God loves me. I know He gave his life for me. I know what God called me to do. I know God has a plan for my life and my future family BUT I had a desire. That desire was a right now desire. Isn't that so typical? We as a generation are overly zealous when it comes to the right now. We want to get rich… right now. We want a car… right now. We want a successful business… right now. We're not even dating, but want to get married… right now. Its foolishness when you think about it. We all know that every good thing takes time and is worth waiting for. That wait period also develops our character and transforms us through experiences so that we are better prepared for the next season. If we got everything we desired right now, we would lose it in little to no time. Patience is truly a virtue, and a fruit of the spirit.

So, call on the Holy Spirit to help you. The great saints of old were admired for their faith and patience when it came to the promises of the Lord. One bible character in particular took the route that I did. In the book of Genesis, Abraham and Sarah decided instead of waiting on the Lord to open Sarah's womb, they would create their own family and have Abraham lie with Hagar to produce Ishmael. This was COMPLETELY outside of the will of God and led to problems down the road.

Friend, learn from Abraham's mistake— learn from my mistake. It's not easy but it's definitely worth it to wait on God. Do you need a miracle from the Lord? Know that He moves in His own timing, not ours. He knows what's best for us and He literally comes right on time. The old folks use to say that all the time and we found it cliché. However, today the words ring so true in my life. At the end of the day we have to realize that He is God and we are not. His will, and not our own will echo into eternity.

Whatever is occupying your mind right now, cast it onto Jesus. Evolve. Evolve from the 'take it into my own hands' mentality and realize Jesus has got you, fam! At times we feel like things won't get done if we don't do them. So not true. You are not that powerful, my friend. Get over yourself. Yes, you! This is a clear sign of pride and conceit. Humble yourself before God and dedicate all of your plans to Him. After all, "A man's mind plans his way [as he journeys through life], But the Lord directs his steps and establishes them (Proverbs 16:9 (AMP))."

Pray: 'God, I cast all of my care onto you. I clear my mind of any and all distractions. I clear my mind of my own selfish gain and ill-motivated desires. Give me the strength God and the wisdom to stop trying to take things into my own hands. Teach my heart that you are God and I am not. Deliver me from pride. Humble me before your throne. Guide my life God, in all circumstances, especially when I do not know what is next.'

7

Kujichagulia

Blank. Bare. Basic.
Empty. Simple. Safe.
They paint small boxes and basic hues of unthreatening colors on my canvas.
They smile and nod and reassure that this way is best,
That I can be just like the rest-
Happily miserable.

They paint with strokes that imply that my destiny
Will somehow get the best of me
But, who wrote it?

Did you give me this vision, bold with neon accent?
Did you swaddle this dream?
Did you author its script?
No.
I define destiny for me.
I define happiness,
And what you believe it to be
Isn't quite what I had in mind.

See, this morning I woke up in the east
And before I could rest for the evening in the west
I came up with a name;
A name for my journey, a name for myself:
Goddess. Queen. Royalty.
She will be called Zuri, beautiful,
Sanaa, a work of art.

See, I title myself for my magical finish

55

And find strength in acknowledging that magic was never my start.
So, I'll speak from my heart,
And I will not slip away
And fade into the bleak background you have on display.
I will create another,
More lively, more striking,
More tantalizing than any work I've ever seen,
Because, who gave me this vision?
Not you or your minions,
Not this world or even my own mind,
But it's a gift from the spirit who eternally lives inside so,

I'll pain from my soul
With truth as my goal.
I'll twirl and whirl in determination and self love
And my brushes will meet the canvas like earth embracing the heavens above
And give to it

Colors,
Deep as the ocean and bold as the horizon
Until the image on this canvas is new and bright
And worthy of its OWN spotlight.

From now until I've grown old
I'll be separate with an unorthodox destiny to hold,
But I'll be smiling,
And unlike the rest, I
will be happy.
Ase.

Kwanzaa is the only official African American holiday. I was not aware of what Kwanzaa was until college. My family always believed, 'if it wasn't Jesus' then we didn't need to know about it.' After attending a historically black university, I learned the beauty behind this holiday. It is an annual holiday that is celebrated from the day after Christmas until the first day of the new year. It focuses on thankfulness, family, and culture.

Kujichagulia (pronounced koo-jee-chah-GOO-lee-ah) is day two of Kwanzaa. In Swahili, kujichagulia means self-determination. According to mydailykwanzaa.wordpress.com, it is "a commitment and practice of defining, defending and developing ourselves instead of allowing or encouraging others to do it." Although rooted in afro-centricity, I believe that can ring true and help to mentally evolve all peoples.

Upon researching, this day of Kwanzaa stood out to me more than any of the others. This could be because at that time I was going through a mental shift and pressing to get free from people bondage (an unhealthy need to please and be measured by other's opinions). I was learning to be my own person independent of what other people thought of me or the boxes they placed me in.

What boxes have you been living in? Are the boxes and labels from your family, friends, and community still keeping you mentally imprisoned? For me, these boxes and labels kept me from dreaming big and living my life to fulfillment. I had to realize that Jesus never allowed people to keep Him mentally tied up or bound. He was free from people bondage.

Jesus was God made flesh and was persecuted by people. Can you imagine that? Jesus! "This High Priest of ours understands our weaknesses, for he faced all of the same tests we do, yet he did not sin" (Hebrews 4:15).

Isaiah 2:22 says, "Don't put your trust in mere humans. They are as frail as breath. What good are they?"

The people who are judging you or trying to get you to change are just like you— a mere human. They breathe just as you do, only for a short time. They are on this earth for a short time and are gone. How do they somehow have power over you They are no one's god. Why are you admiring them and placing your trust in them? Isaiah 2:22 is a very powerful verse. I encourage you to look at this verse in various versions. Study it. Get in down in your soul.

It's like we are allowing people to make us doubt God. We know who He is and who He says we are in Him but somehow our mama's words can turn everything around. Our significant other constantly gets upset and spews hate toward us and we routinely find our self-esteem in pieces. (By the way, that's probably a sign that he or she isn't God's best for you.) Like Job's wife in the Bible, people are asking us to curse God. They are asking us to let go of what God said and somehow distort ourselves to become a version of us that we do not recognize… a version of us that is safer for them!

You're probably reading this and thinking, 'Whew! I don't know who in the world would let people change them like that!' but bro, you do! Think about it. You were really excited about getting your hair done differently. You just knew that it was going to be cute. You make the appointment, go to the bank for the cash, and you're set.

You call your friend to let her know of your plan and she says something shady like, 'I just saw so and so with those. They didn't look right.' Or maybe you're interested in someone. They are really cute and down to earth in your opinion. You show a picture to your homies and they are like, 'Yeah, she's alright.' What? Now your whole opinion, optimism and excitement has been tainted. You may still get your hair done or go on that date with her but your friend's words are still ringing in your head. Why do you trust more in what they say than your own opinion and discernment?

If you look throughout the Bible, there were so many people, including Jesus Christ, who ran into people and their judgement, but they did not allow people to make them feel less than.

If Jesus were afraid of people; if He had put all His trust in the Romans or all His trust in King Herod or Pilate, He could have started thinking that maybe He should change His direction. No!

Stop changing yourself and your direction for people who are as frail as breath. Keep your mind on those things that are heavenly and good. We do not store up our treasures or our hopes on earth. We store them in Heaven; we focus on heavenly things. Why? Because Matthew 6:21 says, "Wherever your treasure is, there the desires of your heart will also be."

One major problem could be who you are talking to. I don't want you to walk away from this chapter feeling like you should disregard any and everything that anyone says to you because they are not God. You should have godly friends that can speak into your life when you need it. Proverbs 12:26 says, "The godly give good advice to their friends; the wicked lead them astray."

At first thought, you could think the wicked are those people at the liquor houses or the family members that you keep at an arm's length but the Bible doesn't say 'only the *obviously* wicked.' Anyone that shuns Christ or refuses to accept Him is more than susceptible to being a vessel for the enemy to use. I know it hurts that that's your mama, your friend, or your boo, but if they are saying Jesus is not the Christ or if they nonverbally say, 'I'm not going to do what it takes to follow, obey and love Jesus,' then they are the wicked this verse speaks of. Their ways are wicked. They have one foot in and one foot out when it comes to God. Jonathan McReynolds makes it clear in his song, "No Gray" that we can't play this in between dance. That goes for us personally, but also for those that we keep closest to us and our confidants.

I've learned that in trying to live righteously, I need community. Yes, it's okay to share your dreams and aspirations, but try to share with those who are choosing to live righteously. As believers in Jesus Christ, we are all righteous because of our faith. It's a different thing to live out that righteousness and be holy. I've taken my dreams or even my decisions to people who denounce Christ and I always get a shaky response.

You cannot be firmly planted in anything other than the Word of God when sharing your heart with others.

Always pray about a decision first. Then when you decide to go to people for advice, make sure it's someone who knows God and knows His Word so that you're not getting a response and advice that's rooted solely in their own opinion and flesh. See? I know they are your friend and that's great. I'm not saying do not take advice from friends who are unbelievers or who are not choosing to live holy. I'm just simply suggesting that you think through the weight you give to their responses. This is where we again have to ask ourselves the question, 'Are we putting our trust in God or man?'

When we choose to confide in other believers, we know their response may come through them but it will align with the Word and what God has already told us. This way, God is in every aspect of our decision making.

Before going to someone with your vision, look at their fruit. Are they wicked? Are they following the Lord? Does their life reflect where I want to be in some way, shape or form? If it does, how did they get there? Was it by God? A lot of times it's not hard to know someone's motives or who or what they worship. Just listen to their conversation. What is in you, (whatever you meditate on) will come out. Is everything that comes out of their mouth secular? If they have success, did they get it in a moral way? If not, are you willing to sacrifice your God, Jesus Christ, in order to get what they have? If the answer is no, don't confide in them. Their opinion can be valuable but not if it's going to cost you your peace or deter you from what God has told you to do. We go running to mentors and people who have accomplished what we are striving for but remember God authored your gifts and talents. He will steer your desires. Don't get too wrapped up in people who look like or seem like they have it made. Always consult Jesus first because they are only human.

For me, I went through a season where my cousin Nish was the only phone number, I allowed myself to dial. I had to protect my dreams and my visions from the opinions of people. Jesus was fully God and fully man. He succeeded at being a champion despite the people. I, on the other hand, needed some separation to still my heart, clear my mind, and focus on God. It's cool to keep friends close but your Bible has to be kept closer. Its words bring life and power.

Through power, Jesus overcame the enemy on multiple accounts. We should not be afraid of the enemy unless we do not have the power of the Holy Spirit within us. If you have the power of the Holy Spirit within you, you are able to stand up and speak to the devil, his minions, that power you are wrestling against and say, 'Flee! Get away from me in the name of Jesus! I decree and declare that you will no longer come in this house. You will not take over my son. You will not take over my daughter. You will not take over my mind. You will not creep up in my job. I cast you down right now in the name of Jesus and I better not see you back here again!' You have to learn to bind some things in prayer. We often wrestle and struggle with our mindset because we've allowed our mind to be a playground; public property for the wicked.

Change your mindset concerning people and the enemy. Don't be concerned with whether or not other people believe like you do or believe in you. You don't need a cosigner to your faith.

A true test of character is when you indubitably say no to compromise; that's tenacity of character. Tenacious people will not quit, much like persistent people. Persistent people keep going until they succeed. Tenacious people do the same, however, tenacity is different in that it adapts its methods to accomplish a goal. Adapt. Evolve.

Come to a resolve that you will do what the Lord is telling you to do whether you have fans or friends or no one at all. Know that God is your audience. Know that God is your friend. If you need to take a step away from certain people who you know have a 'big voice' in your mind and decisions, do that. If you need to fast from social media or delete some of the accounts you follow that try to 'encourage you' but actually make your dreams feel inferior or out of reach, do that. Protect your mind and all that it produces so that you can follow your OWN path to your OWN success.

Pray: 'God, I pray for tenacity and determination. I pray for a boldness to chase after you with everything that is in me. Free me from the opinions of others and lead to me people who are striving to seek you and be more like you. In Jesus' name. Amen.'

8

Two Steps Back

I take *two steps back and throw my hands up,*

Hands that were once cuffed by sin,
Habits, people, and thought processes that always seemed to win.

I give up.
I throw in the towel.
I want to run away to start over somehow.

In life we all play the leading role
And I'm the leading lady in a film bought with a price
Then sold,
Not for riches or for gold,
But for self idolatry and strongholds
And now I'm the leading lady in a film with a script
And production I cannot control.

I take two steps back and hang my head down.
My life is flipped and turned around.
I thought I was the director,
And I thought I controlled the cast.
I'm searching for answers as friends are leaving
And the audition room is filled with toxic people from my past.

So, I'm taking two steps back.

I need direction, I need vision;

I need joy, I need love;

I need to make a decision.

But in a time like this, who can you trust?
I mean, who do you trust when the you, you thought you knew
Goes up in dust?

Well, I'm here to tell you there's a savior.
Not a man with flawed behavior,
Not a man who will give you a stage,
Or lights, camera, action and a raise.

But a God whose foresight is greater.
He created the heavens and designed the earth.
He knew your name—
Your hopes and disasters at birth,
And he's holding your hand.
Love, this is not the end.
It's a tragic cliffhanger in a brilliantly written saga.

So, take two steps back and throw your hands up in surrender
To the one God bigger than doubts and fears.
He'll take the lead.
To the one God eternal and already here.
He'll take the lead.
To the one God with a plan that he'll make clear.
He'll take the lead.
You don't have to cast another.

God is talking to you, but are you listening? At this point in our mental and spiritual journey, we want to be more like Jesus. We want to know His voice. We want to seek Him for wisdom and insight. We keep asking for the Lord to speak to us, change us, and fill us with His Spirit but when He speaks, we ignore him and argue. He may say, "Fast." Our response is, "Well, Lord, I don't know about that. I can't go without meat. It's Christmas. I need my social media for my birthday or for this event that is coming up." You see the issue? Imagine God was an earthly father. Any man or person would be like, "Yo! Why would I continue to try to help you when you're not even listening or trying to consider what I'm saying?!" It's like when you ask someone what they want to eat and they say, 'Anything.' You suggest Arby's and they're like, "Ew, nah, I don't want that." "Okay! So why did you ask me?!"

God is saying, "You want to know my voice. You want to be closer to me. You want to know how to go deeper in worship. I am telling you but you're holding on so tightly to yourself, your pride and your soul (where your mind, emotions, and earthly passions lie)." We are holding on so much to that identity. We won't let it go and be completely transformed by the Holy Spirit. We won't let Him change the way we think. He saves us so that He can change us. 2 Corinthians 5:17 says, "This means that anyone who belongs to Christ has become a new person. The old life is gone; a new life has begun!" You can't pack a suitcase and bring the old into your new life. Spiritual seasons shift.

I've been through spiritual shifts before. I've seen seasons change in my life. I can look back over my life and pinpoint shifts and changes that the Lord brought me through, but every time I gave the Lord pushback. It's difficult and uncomfortable to do something that will change you but if the Lord is calling you to it, do it! It is disrespectful to tell the Lord that He has to wait until we can see things clearly and until we understand what He is trying to do before we give him the okay to move in our lives. It sounds completely insane to tell the God of the universe that your way is better.

If you simply choose to walk with God, I promise He will lead you. Listen to His voice. We don't listen because we believe all our ways are clean and innocent. "Do I really need to fast, Lord? The way I eat isn't that bad." "Do I really need to stop listening to secular music in this season, God? The music I listen to is pretty motivational and culturally aware." No. Stop making excuses and talking back to God.

We have to mentally evolve to a place of maturity that says we are not the lead nor the producer of our own show. We do not write the script. God does. We have to rest in surrender to Him.

Proverbs 16:2 says, "People may be pure in their own eyes, but the Lord examines their motives." God knows where all of our decisions are rooted. He is protecting us from ourselves. You want to contact that person out of pride. You want to start that business out of idolatry. You want to post that picture because of low self-esteem. You want to wear that because of lust. You want to listen to that because of your attachment to depression. God is protecting us from ourselves. He is protecting us from wickedness and evil that so easily trips us up. If we listen to His voice and follow Him, He will let us rest and lead us "beside peaceful streams." The Bible says so in Psalms 23.

Listening to God's voice is not some spooky thing. It's not hard. It's only hard if you are not in His presence and in His Word. You can't know a person's voice if you're never around them or speak to them. Practically, read God's Word and get to know his character. Pray to Him. After you pray to Him, don't just get up and go about your day. This is why it's so important not to just pray to God on your lunch break or in your car. Pray to him then sit in His presence. Try to clear your mind of any and everything that tries to creep in. Don't think about kids, your mama, your job, how much you need to clean up... nothing. This is where worship comes in. Focus on God. Think about how big He is. Think about how infinite He is. Imagine Him in Heaven on His throne. Think of how He's moving in that room, in your heart. Think of His thoughts. What is He thinking toward you? How deep is His love? How powerful is He? How strong is He? How smart and wise is He?

Worshipping God for who He is, not what He has done, is to know God. That kind of communion with Him draws you closer to him. Mentally toss everything else aside and focus on Him. He will speak to you.

God's voice will save you from so many wrong decisions, wrong people, and wrong circumstances. If you're reading this and you're like, "Inez, I'm already in the wrong circumstance. It's too late." Know that it's never too late.

God will rescue you once you choose to get back to Him. We

often times find ourselves in wickedness and darkness but we can't worry about evil people. We have to believe that God is with us, even in our little. He will rescue us.

Psalms 37:23 says, "The Lord directs the steps of the godly. He delights in every detail of their lives." God has not forgotten about you though you are going through or going under. He is paying attention to everything that you are doing, every detail of your life. He takes joy in that pivotal moment that we decide to choose Him. When you choose Him, he shows up right there. Now if we are just chilling, swimming, backstroking in our mess, and that's what we want, we have free will and God will allow you to carry on. But when we decide to just straight bolt toward God through our grief, and promiscuity, and addictions, and depression, and anxieties, and choose the peace of God, He will show up right when it seems like it's almost too late. Verse 24 of that same chapter, Psalms 37 says, "Though they stumble, they will never fall, for the Lord holds them by the hand." No matter how dark it may look, how hard it is, no matter how close death may seem, you're never going to fall if you are godly. If you're trusting and believing in God, it is possible to stumble and trip a little but you won't fall because God is holding you by the hand. How intimate is that?

Think of a child that is learning to walk. They have a parent standing over them holding both of their hands as they step. At this point, they aren't really walking. They are stumbling most of the way but they won't fall because that parent is holding them by the hand.

We often do not expect to be saved? For many of us, life has made us jaded. We've been mentally, emotionally and sometimes physically abused to the point that we don't believe in a Savior who will hold our hand. The only 'saviors' we've seen be successful in our lives are superheroes in the movies. We tried a man or a woman and they failed to save us. We tried our parents and they failed to save us. We tried our siblings and they failed to save us. We tried that job and money and both failed to save us. We tried alcohol and it failed to save us. We tried weed and it failed to save us. But you know what? None of those things or people created you. None of those things or people are omniscient enough to know your past, where your present stems from, and your future.

Trust God. He is the only Savior that is worth it. Trust me. I totally know. My life has been more than a mess. More than abuse. More than addiction. More than depression. More than hopelessness… at its start. Aren't you glad Jesus doesn't just leave you at the starting line? He will pick you up and carry you on toward something greater than you could ever imagine. Your future is greater than you could ever imagine. You are greater than you could ever imagine.

This is awesome news but we don't just trust God because we believe He will bring us out. We don't just find peace because things will turn out the way we want them to. No. We trust God and find peace because we know His Will, will be done. His Will may have some hardships or sharp turns but those hardships and turns are always there to make us better and develop us into the people that can carry the weight of His purpose for our lives. We have to make a stand, not for our own desires, but for God's Will and plan for our lives. Our worth is not in man but in pleasing God. People may get angry or not understand your decision.

They may fire back at you. They might trip you up. They may upset you or throw you a little off your game but trust me when I say, you will not fall. God is so close He is holding you by the hand. You can't fail because God cannot fail. Remember that we don't fail when we are being godly because God is delighting in every detail of our lives. He's proud of us when we are walking as we should. All we have to do is acknowledge Him and relinquish our will and know that 'Hey, God. You got me.'

Things may not work out the way you want them to but accept and be okay with God's Will being done. Take joy in that. Peace comes from knowing and trusting his Will is best. When God sees that trust, your last prayer, your cries on your knees, your whispers of the name Jesus, He will find you. He will show up. He will blow your mind. Have faith.

Faith isn't simply believing that something is true. So believing that God will come through, that He will deliver you, that He will save and help you, that He will turn the situation around, fix that money situation, bring you a spouse… believing it to be true is just the first step. The second step to faith is acting on that belief. You can believe that Santa is real. You can believe the stories of Santa are true. You actually baking cookies and sitting them out and not buying any presents because you believe Santa is going to bring them— that's faith. Anyone can say they believe something but faith is actually acting on what you believe. We say we believe God loves us and that we are worthy but we cower in the face of adversity and criticisms of others. Have childlike faith. Believe and trust that God will do what he says he's going to do. Allow that faith to guide your decisions and the way you move.

Pray: Lord, Help me to hear your voice. Settle my mind so that I may focus on you. I know you will never let me fall. God, it's your Will that I prosper so lead me, God. Teach me your voice. Teach me how to worship you in silence. Teach me how to have faith in noise. In Jesus name, Amen.

9

I Am

We confuse <u>who</u> we are with <u>where</u> we are.

Being down does not make me a failure.
Having money in my pocket does not make me poor.
Being angry does not make me bitter
And success does not make you better.

We are all flawed.
Flawed beautifully.
But we all must be strong.
Mentally.

I may have played the fool but I'm no idiot.
The secret is understanding who you are no matter the situation,
Understanding your growth no matter the allegation.
People cannot hurt you,
They can only attempt.
You decide.

And today,
I decided that I am prosperous
Even though this economy isn't built for us.
I am rich-
In grace, in laughter,
In knowledge and faith ever after.

I am woman. I am strong. I am black.
I am the manifestation of every dream you let die;

Every dream you gave up on that shriveled and never grew wings to grace the sky.
I am power. I am light.
I am the sweet, still song of the universe at night.

I am.
Because He is.
And he is not the author of confusion,
So I'm convinced your idea of me is just an allusion.

I am.
Because He is.
And that is eternal.

Find rest.

Our thoughts are oftentimes wrapped up in this world and what it deems to be important. We go day in and day out living by the world's standards. You go to work because the world says it's important. You go to school because the world says it's important. You go to church because the world says you'll get 'brownie points' with Jesus. You indulge yourself in unhealthy things and go to unholy places because the world says 'you deserve to have a good time.' YOLO, right? Our friends, who don't know who they are in Christ, encourage these things with absolutely no idea who God has called you to be. You ignore the person God has called you to be until Sunday morning, then for the rest of the week you are the person that this world, these people, find acceptable.

A lot of your mental bondage is coming from the expectations of others. You say you know who you are and what you want for yourself but you're actually trying to measure up against others. If not that, you're measuring up against someone's idea of you.

Maybe you're the eldest in your family. Maybe you're the only one who accepts Jesus as your Savior, for real, for real. Maybe you've achieved a lot of firsts in your family such as the first to go to college. People expect you to be the strong one, and you are. But these pressures and expectations people have for you lead you to try to be your own hero.

God is the only one who can save us, who can make a pathway through the wilderness and create rivers in the dry wasteland (Isaiah 43:19). You're mentally stressed and drained because you're taking on the weight of trying to correct your life and make it better all in your own strength. That's a God job.

How did you get to this place?

Anything that you meditate on is in you and it's going to come out. That's why the Bible tells us to meditate on the Word of God. In Psalms 119:11 David says, "I have hidden your word in my heart, that I might not sin against you." The Bible also says in Proverbs 4:23 to "guard your heart above all else, for it determines the course of your life." But what's in your heart? What have you been meditating on? For a lot of us, we meditate on comparison, people bondage, pride, materialism, selfishness and self-righteousness. We are medicating on our past and the person it has led us to be. "Well, I'm this way because my parents weren't there to protect me when I was young. I'm this way because this person did this to me in high school. I'm this way because I'm the one in my family that has to make it." I hear you but <u>we cannot 'save' ourselves</u>. Believing that you can is self-idolatry. It is pride. Harsh, I know. Boasting in your self-idolatry and finding reasons to justify it doesn't change what it is. You've allowed your circumstances to dictate the way you think, the pressure you put on yourself, and the pressures you allow from others.

Jesus has forgotten your past. He has worked it all for your good. Why are you still holding on to it and meditating on its residue?

If you're filling up or meditating on this world and your carnal circumstances, then you are being filled with the love of the world. 1 John 2:15 says, "Do not love this world nor the things it offers you, for when you love the world, you do not have the love of the Father in you." This doesn't mean you're evil or love the devil, it just means that your thoughts and meditations are not properly focused. We are called to live by faith. You cannot live by what your eyes see.

Getting too caught up in what you see leads to a hazy picture of who you are. You are power. You are light. You are a child of God. We forget these things. This is how we leave room for the enemy to come in. We run to be who mama or daddy wants us to be. We leave who God says we are to make ourselves feel worth it on this earth. We create our own twisted identity through works of the flesh, negative thought patterns, pride, and comparison. We operate through flesh and flesh fails us every time. This leads to depression because we are disappointed in who the world says we are or who we end up becoming… that day. Yes, that day, because that feeling of pride or brief happiness fades quick.
Only the joy of the Lord lasts. Only what the Lord has spoken over you will last.

Yes, we are free and free indeed. Yes, we laid out at the altar. Yes, we cried all night to Jesus but we are human. Somehow, no matter how many times God rescues us, our thoughts seem to forget the goodness of God. Your first go to, especially if you have not mentally evolved from the hurts of your past, is to rescue yourself. What does that look like? Getting your hair done. Going on trips. Shopping. Spending money on unnecessary things.

Drinking and going out. We do these things to make ourselves feel better. We try to rescue ourselves from our bad day and situations but anytime our focus is not on God, we are going to lose. Time-fillers materialism and distractions are ways the world addresses negative circumstances.

But we, being evolved, are not of this world. Your thoughts and your mindset have to be out of this world because your source is out of this world. Know that you are bomb. Speak it. Your talents are out of this world

Put your hope and stock in heavenly things and not of this world. Know who you are. The spirit of God is who leads you, not your flesh, folks' opinions, or your mama's expectations. If you are feeling confused about who you are, know that God is not the author of confusion. In order to evolve into a resolve about who we are we first have to check how we are measuring our worth.

What makes you feel worth it? What makes you feel important? What gives you comfort? If the answer is anything carnal, meaning something you can run to the world for, we have a problem. However, it's a problem we can solve. We can evolve.

When you realize that you are running to a movie theater to get your mind off of the day (escape-ism) or running to wine to relax or running to google to decide or running to people to whine, STOP. Call out your flesh and your negative patterns. These patterns are engraving distrust and dysfunction in your psyche. Interrupt your normal.

You may be thinking, 'Inez, I'm realizing that I say I know who I am and I find my identity in Christ but I actually find it in other's opinions and positive comments about me. I actually find it in clothes or my car or my home. I find it in money. I find it in friends. I find it in what job I have or my spouse or partner. How do I reverse all of that?'

You've confused who you are with where you are and what you have. Friend, when you feel you have lost your identity along the way the only one that can help is Jesus. Maybe you never even picked up your new identity at the foot of the cross where you laid your sins down. Jesus' grace and mercy can help you find you because He knows exactly where you left you. God created you and He knows every thought you have. You cannot hide from God. Remember in the last chapter we learned that the Word says He examines your motives and intentions. If you're not sure exactly where you've lost your identity or where it may be hidden, pray to God and ask Him to reveal things to you. Ask that God make you sensitive to His spirit as well as thought patterns and habits that are not edifying.

Pray: Lord, I thank you for opening my spiritual eyes to who I am in you. I thank you that when I accepted you as my Lord and Savior, you gave me a new identify. The old has passed away and behold all things are new. Help all things to be new in my life. I denounce my allegiance to sin and sinful thinking. I curse all negative thought patterns and behaviors. I say they have no place in my present or future. I speak life over myself and my mind. I am power. I am light. I am righteous. I am wholly loved by my Father God in

Heaven. I am rich. I am prosperous. I am successful. I am beautiful. I am strong. My identity in my father is eternal. Give me rest, Jesus. Give my mind rest concerning who I am and my purpose. You alone can rescue me and lead me in peace. I trust you, Lord. I know that what you speak over me is greater than anything I could create for myself. Help me be meek, Father. I want to learn you, thus learning who I truly am. I love you Jesus and I know it is done. Amen.

10

Fireworks

She
She was beautiful and spontaneous
And her colors were miraculous
All stood in awe
As her charisma would burst and her laughter would echo in the night sky
Much like the boom heard on the Fourth of July
She was valiance.
She was grace.
In a crowd she was always the brightest face
That commanded attention
And brought you to your knees.
Her burden was light.

She lit up the night sky
She was beautiful and a muse
That's why you thought to make your move. Huh?
You thought now was the perfect time to invade and intercede
Because after all, she was exactly what you need
She was miraculous
She could work wonders
Her light and her BOOM could overshadow your thunder
The crackle of your lightning and the haziness of your clouds
Could be clothed in her charisma and shine
And your mama would be so proud so,

You held her tight.
You pulled her from the sky
And tried to make her light only shine for your eyes.
In the midst of your storm you positioned her on the ground
Cold, no light. No colors. No crowd.

FIREWORKS

And you were happy
To have her glow and her warmth by your side.
Her grace was now your grace
And you didn't have to hide.

While others scream they are happy for you
And say you've done well
You forgot to look inside you
And clean out all the hell.

You can't go looking for someone to remedy your flaws
You have to put in the work yourself
And the only one who could ever help
Is Christ, the one who died for all

And see, she's just not that tall.
She's not that eminent, that's not her call.
She's meant to be in the sky bursting
But here, with you, she's suffocating.
Her light is growing dim and her magic is rendering powerless
She's uncomfortable and hurting,
Her tears are countless.

You don't know how to nurture this fire. You don't
know how to grow this flame.
You, my brotha, are exactly the same
As every other man that tries to pull her from the sky
Thinking her color are all that she has inside
But you don't understand her.

You'll never understand the grace and joy that is found in a flame,
The freedom of dancing wildly in the sky
Until you start your journey to the same,

And light your own soul.

I had a friend sit me down and say, "Yeah, sis. You gotta stop doing that."

We were at dinner and I was sharing reflections of my past relationship. I found that although I had mentally evolved, I still had a lot more evolving to do when it came to men and love. Love is such a complicated thing. We have twisted and turned it in so many directions that it looks nothing like the Father's love.

I explained to my friend that my love for this 'X' was totally unhealthy. It was more of an attachment to a 'project' I had been working on for so long. See, he was my project. He actually knew he was a project. His line to get back in my life stated such. He said, sitting across the table from me at dinner, "I've grown so much and I feel that you are the only woman that should reap the benefits of the man I've become." Brotha really felt that he had grown, thanks to my help in some way, shape, or form, and wanted to tell me, just so I could get in on this 'good man rarity' because I deserved my paycheck. I deserved to be repaid for all I had poured into him and all I endured while waiting for him to become this man.

Chile, if you aren't careful— if you don't evolve past the point of dependency on men and <u>pride</u>— you will find yourself exactly where I ended up; back in the arms of a man who wants only to take from me. This dude viewed me as a genie in a bottle or some kind of golden ticket that could inspire him and make him, somehow, what he was not: a God-fearing, happy, fruitful man.

The same can go for guys. Don't allow some woman to walk into your life with heels and lipstick that doesn't have anything more to offer you. Love does not take and take and take. Love is sacrificial.

Think about God's love for us. Man, that's perfect love. His love edifies us and sees us in a way that we can't even see ourselves. He's patient with us. Instead of taking, He gives us peace and a promise. He's devoted to us and our plans. He wants to see us prosper and does all that He can to make sure that happens.

See the difference between true, unblemished love and the pride-centered situation I was in?

Stop letting your pride, emotions, and flesh choose partners for you. We will lay out and cry, "Lord, I surrender all!" but one area that we always keep hold of and try to control is our romantic relationships.

I can remember the exact moment that God snatched me from that way of thinking and reminded me to cast ALL my cares on him and submit all that I do to him.

One night, I was on Instagram scrolling. I was seeing my friends' new relationships and some Instagram models. They were fine! I was like, "Yo! I want my husband to look like this!" I started thinking about Xs. When I say 'X' I really mean people who have an 'X' on them because they didn't work out or our relationship wasn't serious enough to consider for the long-term, but that night, I started thinking about reviving those interactions.

I know some of y'all have been there. I started going down this mental rabbit-hole. Just then, God spoke to my heart, Jeremiah 2:11. My first thought was the scripture Jeremiah 29:11; "'For I know the plans I have for you,' says the LORD." I was like "Yes, Lord! That's what I need to hear! You have something (a man) greater for ME!" But really, God was trying to give me a check in my spirit.

Jeremiah 2:11-13 actually says in part, "Has any nation ever traded its gods for new ones….. worthless idols! The heavens are shocked at such a thing… They have abandoned me— the fountain of living water. And they have dug for themselves cracked cisterns that can hold no water at all!"

Whoa. What I took away from that is that it was so stupid of me to think I could place another god before Him— literally speaking, placing another man or person that I see before God. Ideally, I should have been reading my Word but instead I was up staring at Instagram models. I could have been praying to God or worshipping but instead I'm up debating whether or not I should text this person that I use to sin with that did me wrong or in some capacity hurt me. This was a person that I tried to build with out of my own might instead of choosing to consult God. And here I was again, in my own strength, trying to reach out to some dude from my past.

See, I was doing exactly what the bible was speaking of in Jeremiah 2:11-13. I was trading the glory that I have in Christ for a worthless idol. I'm trading what God has planned and in store for me for a worthless idol. In doing so, I was rejecting God and abandoning Him for this worthless thing. Isn't God so much greater? Why am I choosing what I can do instead of his perfect Will?

So, number one, I was rejecting God. The second thing that was crazy to me was that I was trying to dig my own well. A broken well! I was digging out a cracked cistern that might look good on the outside but it can't hold any water at all. God is a fountain of living water that washes me new everyday but I'm rejecting him and saying, "Nah, I'm gonna build my own." But what I'm going to build, the Bible is already telling me, is going to be cracked and broken.

So, what was I doing? What are you doing? We have a tendency to try to do things in our own strength. Even though God has told us multiple times we are in a hidden season, we start to get impatient— "But Jesus, I don't want to wait. Look at that person. They have theirs. What about me?" and all the while, you don't even know what your next step in life is. You're worried about what someone's relationship looks like, wanting to pull a man into your life when your life isn't even centered. You haven't done what God has told you to do to achieve and conquer personal goals.

I was thinking that from my loneliness (an emotion that we should not be led by) I could dig my own well that's not going to bear me anything at all.

A well or cistern is meant to hold water so that later on when you are thirsty or in need you can pull from it and be satisfied. If its cracked or broken, how are you going to pull from it?

The Bible says it won't hold any water at all but here you are just digging. There's no love you're going to get from it. There's no peace you're going to get from it. There's no real eternal satisfaction you're going to get from it. There's no life that you're going to gain because you're doing it in your own strength. Instead, stay right where you are, planted with your glorious God. He's the fountain of living water. You'll never be thirsty. You will always be satisfied. You will always have a well from which to pull life.

I joined an organization for women at the end of 2016 that is dedicated to serving and pleasing God with their bodies and their whole life. After joining this organization, I decided to submit all that I am to Jesus. What does that practically look like? I started wearing a ring on my left ring finger. It symbolizes my devotion to Christ and His devotion to me. It is an external expression of my heart posture toward God. I submit to Him, I am led by Him, I consult Him in all things. He is my husband and I am his bride. Isn't that how it's supposed to be? Aren't we, the church, the people, the bride of Christ?

Needless to say, I was so on fire for God when I purchased that first ring (I've had a few). As time went on, however, and I started to get unsolicited opinions from others and doubt started to creep in. Besides people just scoffing or laughing or being sarcastic when addressing my reasoning for wearing the ring, the most impactful response that brought about doubt was, "How are you going to find a husband if they think you are already married?"

That thing got me to thinking. "What if men don't approach me because of this ring? How will my husband find me?

Is he trifling if he approaches a woman with a ring on her finger? Do I really want a man that would be bold enough to approach a woman who at first glance looks married?"

You see how the enemy finds open doors and uses conversations to plant seeds of doubt? This is why I stressed in an earlier chapter to guard your heart from people and words. They can be seeds especially if you struggle with anxiety just as I do. But because I had spent months and years on my face with Jesus learning to mentally rise above obsessive thoughts and learning how to stay grounded and planted in God's truth, I was able to push past opinions and doubt.

Whatever God said He's going to do; He's going to do. I have to truly believe and trust that the person God is bringing to me is not going to be deterred by a ring on my finger. The person that is supposed to see the ring and walk away will see the ring and walk away. The person who is supposed to know what it represents will know. Who's for me will come despite something as small as a ring. I kept my ring on my left ring finger and wear a ring today. I continued to show the world that I trust God and I'll live for God. I'll do whatever He's asking me to do, even if it doesn't make sense to you. Who are you? My friend? My aunt? My mom? You are frail as breath (Isaiah 2:22) and your opinions are fleeting but God is eternal. Don't allow ANYONE— no man, no family member, no friend— to snuff out your fire for God.

How do we practically do that? How do we change our mindset about relationships and love? Well first, friend, stop fornicating. Yes, I used that churchy word... fornicating. Fornication is any sexual act outside of the bounds of marriage.

Now that we have accepted Jesus as our personal Savior and have evolved to a place of viewing ourselves differently, we must start to seek Jesus and righteous living. If you don't feel that you're there yet, skip the remainder of this chapter! Seriously. I'm not trying to play the role of the Holy Spirit. It is His job to lead you and guide you and empower you as you continue to walk with Him and grow closer to Him.

For the rest of us, I am urging you to stop having sex because sex is so much bigger than the physical, flesh to flesh. It's a spiritual encounter. There's no way to get closer to an individual than to have sex with them. It's more than intimacy. It was designed by God to make two people one flesh. It's beautiful within its bounds: marriage.

Take a vow of celibacy. Find friends that are truly living for God that won't pull you away from Him. No, not a friend of the opposite sex. At least not yet. That's too much temptation and your mentality has not evolved to a place to go there yet. Of course, I'm only speaking to people who are really struggling in this area and are determined to live for God and allow Him to change the way they think about love and relationships. Celibacy is only the first step. See, this isn't some sort of behavioral changing, magic potion. God is more concerned about your heart, your purpose on this earth, and your eternal destiny more than he is concerned about your actions. Once you make up your mind that you're not going to have sex anymore, read the Word of God. What does it say about sex? Why should we not have sex? Check to see if those same pastors and preachers you found and listened to in Chapter 3 have any teaching on this matter. They probably do. Get an understanding.

Practically, find people within your church that are in the same boat as you. Maybe your church has a singles ministry you can join to have these difficult conversations. Those singles may inspire you. If your church doesn't have that available, reach out to other Christians your age and pick their brains. What is their mindset toward sex and celibacy? If it's not biblical or Godly, of course turn away but I believe when we seek God and seek Him with our whole hearts, He will be found by us. "If you seek him, you will find him" (1 Chronicles 28:9). There is no excuse. I use to say all the time that I didn't have any friends with the same mindset as me. That was only because I was sitting at home on my butt pouting and complaining. God will lead you. He literally told me which organization to go join. From that organization, I started going to annual conferences focused on devoting your life and body to God. I joined another group of millennial Christians who believe fully in the Holy Spirit. I also began volunteering at a Christian pregnancy care center with the women I met through the organization. We had bible studies together and one even became my roommate!

God will be found by you when you look for him. Plain and simple. These environments that you find yourself in and the people God will surround you with will slowly start to change your mindset toward God, sex, and marriage. I personally did not have any tangible examples or any raw conversations about these things prior to me actually stepping out and finding them. Don't use your ignorance toward the Bible or the ignorance of your parents as an excuse as to why you cannot have a godly standard when it comes to relationships and marriage. Evolve.

Pray: Lord, give me guidance concerning Godly friends and relationships. I no longer want to try to do things my way. I surrender the area of relationships to you, God. I know that your leading is way better than anything I could do myself. Heal me, O God, from past relationships and break soul ties. I am free from soul ties— dependency— in the name of Jesus. Wash me, God. Transform my mind so that I may be able to live out Godly standards. Keep me strong and confident in your Word. Let no one sway me for God, you are with me. I believe in you and your power. I am done making excuses and falling into the same patterns. I am seeking you, O God. Be found by me. In Jesus' name. Amen.

11

Prevail

All things are working.
All things are growing.
All things are progressing.
All things are hoping
Never failing
Never ceasing
Never dying
Because He never fails.
His grace never ceases.
His love never dies
So, what is my ailment?
What is my trial to a God who knows all,
Keeps all,
Prevails over all?
Nothing.

Peace and joy come in knowing
It's working for my good
I'm growing, I'm progressing,
In all things
Trusting and hoping.
I am victorious
He never fails
And I won't fail Him.

God has predestined and called you to a mighty purpose according to Romans 8:29-30 (AMP). The beautiful thing is that His Word says this a few chapters later: "For the gifts and the calling of God are irrevocable [for He does not withdraw what He has given, nor does He change His mind about those to whom He gives His grace or to whom He sends His call" (Romans 11:29 (AMP)). His mind cannot change toward you. He won't take back the call. He won't take away His blessings nor the things He has graced you to do. We get afraid. We get afraid that God is just like man and that He will somehow let us down or be spiteful.

Please rest in knowing that God will NEVER change. NEVER. He's too holy and perfect to let us down.

Once I took hold of that truth I started to walk different and see my life differently. My heart posture changed. I started to filter all of my thoughts and decisions through that lens. GOD CANNOT CHANGE. No matter what the situation looks like, God called me to a purpose. If He won't change His mind, neither will I. God wants to prosper me. God wants to give me a future filled with hope. God wants peace and prosperity for me more than I do! After all, my life was His idea, His plan, not mine.

You have to take back your thought life! Stop allowing the storms and haziness of life's seasons to keep you from knocking on doors God promised He would open. Do not give up on the process. Salvation is a process of evolution. The amazing thing is knowing that the battle is won and you WILL have victory- over anxiety, depression, isms, self-esteem, insecurity, oppression, worry, doubt, fear, suffering, and your past. You will prevail in the end and as your reward, you will receive a heavenly crown.

Pray your own prayer to God as you complete this book. Whatever God has laid on your heart as you read, ask Him to bring it to your remembrance and lead you to what He would have you to do next. Follow His voice.

About the Author

Inez V. Walls is a Christian writer, poet, and speaker from Mooresville, NC. She is a 2015 graduate of The North Carolina Central University in Durham, NC and is the entrepreneur of *Crowned*, a Christian business founded on faith that provides poems, positive and inspirational quotes, devotionals, speaking engagements, poetry performances, tutoring, books, and merchandise. Her writings, performances and speeches are known for their Afro centric and spiritual lenses. Her rhythmic speaking and gentle presentation bring warmth and wisdom to her audiences. Inez believes she is purposed to teach and has found her creative writing as the most raw and effective way to teach of God's love and sovereignty in all circumstances

www.ingramcontent.com/pod-product-compliance
Lightning Source LLC
Chambersburg PA
CBHW020945090426
42736CB00010B/1276